COSTUME CAMEOS 2

by Hazel Ulseth & Helen Sha

Published by  HOBBY HOUSE P
Cumberland, Maryland

ISBN: 087588-201-3

© 1983 by Hazel Ulseth & Helen Shannon
2nd printing April 1985

FRONT COVER: Pattern #9957 adapted from the *Delineator* 1898 and bonnet in size 19in (48.3cm). The dress is a pompadour style, with short, puffed sleeves, fitted slightly high waistline and "frill" caps or bretelles including a fully gathered skirt trimmed with lace and tucks. Pattern may be used with a guimpe. See COSTUME CAMEO 1 for a guimpe pattern. A VICTORIAN CHILD'S BONNET is included in each size.
LEFT: 19in (48.3cm) Tete Jumeau, French bisque on ball-jointed body, paper weight brown eyes, closed mouth, human hair wig, the mark is incised in bisque. Doll is wearing the COSTUME CAMEO 2 dress and bonnet described.
RIGHT: 19in (48.3cm) EJ, French bisque on ball-jointed body, paper weight blue eyes, closed mouth, human hair wig, the mark E 9 J is incised in bisque. Doll is wearing the COSTUME CAMEO 2 dress and bonnet described.

TABLE OF CONTENTS

Styles for Dolls

THE BUTTERICK PUBLISHING CO. LONDON AND NEW YORK.
THE DELINEATOR.

Baby Dolls' Set No. 201 — Consisting of Slip, Skirt and Pinning-Blanket: 7 sizes. Lengths, 12 to 24 inches Any size, 7d. or 15 cents.

Baby Dolls' Set No. 192. Consisting of a Short Dress, Petticoat and Sack: 7 sizes. Lengths, 12 to 24 inches.

Baby Dolls' Set No. 173.—Consisting of a Dress, Sack and Cap: 7 sizes. Lengths, 12 to 24 inches. Any size, 7d. or 15 cents.

Girl Dolls' Set No. 212.—Consisting of a Dress, Empire Coat or Jacket and Mother Goose Hat: 8 sizes. Lengths, 14 to 28 inches. Any size, 7d. or 15 cents.

Girl Dolls' Set No. 195.— Consisting of a Coat and Bonnet: 7 sizes. Lengths, 12 to 24 inches.

Girl Dolls' Set No. 193.—Consisting of a Dress and Guimpe: 7 sizes. Lengths, 12 to 24 inches.

Girl Dolls' Set No. 208.—Dress and Bonnet: 7 sizes. Lengths, 12 to 24 inches. Any size, 7d. or 15 cents.

Girl Dolls' Set No. 206.— Consisting of a Dress and Cape: 7 sizes. Lengths, 12 to 24 inches.

Dolls' Set of Underwear No. 189.—Consisting of a Chemise, Drawers and Petticoat: 7 sizes. Lengths, 12 to 24 inches.

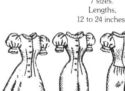

Girl Dolls' Set No. 200.— Consisting of a Bishop Dress and an Empire Jacket: 7 sizes. Lengths, 12 to 24 inches.

Dolls' Set of Combination Undergarments No. 209.— Combination Waist and Drawers and a Combination Waist and Skirt: 8 sizes.

Lady Dolls' Set No. 213.—Consisting of a Russian Dress and Jubilee Toque and Collarette: 7 sizes. Lengths, 16 to 28 inches.

Japanese Lady Dolls' Set No. 114.—Consisting of a Costume: 7 sizes. Lengths, 12 to 24 inches. Any size, 10d. or 20 cents.

Set No. 181.— Costume for a Clown Doll: 7 sizes. Lengths, 12 to 24 inches. Any size, 10d. or 20 cents.

Costume for Santa Claus Doll No. 159.—Consisting of Coat, Vest, Trousers, Leggings and Cap: 7 sizes. Lengths, 12 to 24 inches.

Set No. 182.— Costume for a Jester Doll: 7 sizes. Lengths, 12 to 24 inches.

Set No. 185.—Brownie Doll and Costume: 3 sizes. Lengths, 10, 12 and 14 inches.

Pattern for a Dolls' Body (Designed for Santa Claus and Other Corpulent Dolls): 7 sizes. Lengths (with Head attached), 12 to 24 inches.

Set No. 183.—Costume for a Harlequin Doll: 7 sizes. Lengths, 12 to 24 inches. Any size, 10d. or 20 cents.

ON COSTUME CAMEOS

Our *Costume Cameos I*, published in 1981, and still available, was the forerunner to our book, *Antique Children's Fashions, 1880-1900, A Handbook for Doll Costumers*. This 1981 publication contains a few items which later appeared in the book. *Costume Cameo II* is more or less in the nature of a postscript to the book, as it contains a few ideas which were developed *after* the book was printed.

And it has another pattern, for a dress and bonnet, which we hope will tempt beginning seamstresses, but will prove equally challenging to the advanced costumer.

The dress is from *Delineator*, 1886, and you will love the darling "Victorian" bonnet.

With the burgeoning of reproduction dolls, it appears there will be no let-up for a while in the need for interesting patterns of the correct period for many kinds of dolls. We hope that this booklet will not only fill a need, but will add a little to your knowledge of costuming techniques.

Do make up the little teddy bears after you make the dress and bonnet...your doll will feel less self-conscious if she has something to hold.

...and note, two pairs of shoes, another "perfectly easy bow" as well as a paper doll strip, two pages of antique fashions and lots of other goodies to intrigue you.

SUMMER FROCKS, DELINEATOR 1890s

These charming girls and children are dressed for church in their Sunday best. Note that in the late 1890s natural waistlines were in vogue for misses, with ruffled and bedecked necklines still popular. The younger children still had yoked elaborate neck trim, but otherwise their dresses were simple and all were about knee length. But their hats...what gorgeous creations from the Victorian bonnet (Number 3) and modified mob-type bonnet on Number 1, to the large bows, flowers and lace on the hats of straw.

PETTICOAT & DRAWERS

INSTRUCTIONS FOR MAKING PETTICOAT OR DRAWERS USING COMBINATION OF FRONT WAISTBAND AND DRAWSTRING BACK

Designed for an 18in (45.7cm) doll or larger. All stitch lines, slash lines, and fold lines only are to scale. This pattern may be scaled down for a smaller doll and solves the problem of getting an exact fit around the waist. It also makes underwear more versatile because underwear may be interchanged between dolls.

1. Cut rectangle of size required (see *Antique Children's Fashions, Ill. 21*, p. 77) and a band 1¼in (3.2cm) wide and one-half the length of doll's waist. Fold twice at center backs for placket and sew by hand about 3in (7.6cm), starting at top.
2. Mark center front, center back and side seams (side seams at 1/2 of distance from center front). Slash side seams as shown 1in (2.5cm) from top.
3. Mark a line as shown, between slashes, 5/8in (1.6cm) from top and cut out shaded area.

4. Machine-stitch as shown, two rows of gathering stitches in center area.
5. Pull gathering stitches to exact size of band. Lay band on gathers, right sides together, matching long raw edges and raw edges of band, matching slash. Sew on lower line of gathers. Turn upward.
6. Tack tape for drawstrings at points marked "o." (This tape should be as long as the casing.)
7. To join slashed line and band, fold at slash line along band and make a 1/4in (0.65cm) seam, tapering to a point 1/2in (1.3cm) below gathering stitches. (This stitching will anchor tapes securely.)
8. Turn top edge down 1/4in (0.65cm), then another 3/8in (0.9cm) to form 3/8in (0.9cm) casing. Sew in place, taking special care NOT to catch tape in stitching.
9. Close center back seam to a point 3in (7.6cm) from top. Hem petticoat as desired.

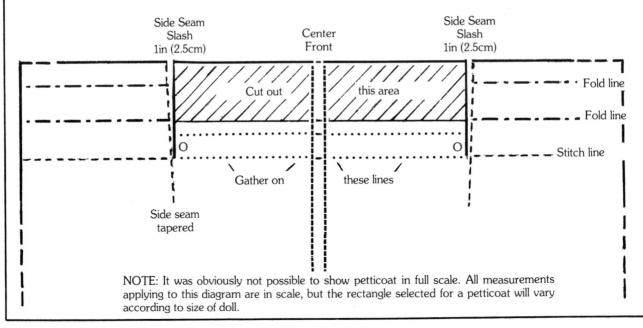

Side Seam Slash 1in (2.5cm) Center Front Side Seam Slash 1in (2.5cm)

Cut out   this area

Fold line
Fold line
Stitch line

O   O

Gather on   these lines

Side seam tapered

NOTE: It was obviously not possible to show petticoat in full scale. All measurements applying to this diagram are in scale, but the rectangle selected for a petticoat will vary according to size of doll.

LITTLE GIRLS' COSTUME

DRESS: Adapted from *Delineator*, 1898, #9957, and presented here in 19in (48.3cm).

The dress is a pompadour style, with short puffed sleeves, fitted slightly high waistline and "frill" caps or bretelles including a fully-gathered skirt trimmed with lace and tucks.

Pattern may be used with a guimpe. See *Cameo I* for a guimpe pattern.

**Throughout this pattern specific references will be made to pages in *Antique Children's Fashions, 1880-1900, A Handbook for Doll Costumers* by Hazel Ulseth and Helen Shannon, for detailed information about some of the sewing techniques used in pattern construction.

For those who are dressing a doll for the first time, it is suggested that assembly instructions and any hints be considered carefully. For ease in doing so, instructions are numbered consecutively for the entire cutting and assembly process.

Front View. **9957**

Back View.

Little Girl's Dress.
(to be worn with or without a guimpe)

Victorian Bonnet
Head size 11½in (29.2cm)

FABRIC REQUIREMENTS

(Fabric requirements for bonnet are not included.)

LINING: About 15in (38.1cm) x 20in (50.8cm).
DRESS: 27in (68.6cm) x 36in (91.4cm) *or* 18in (45.7cm) x 45in (114.3cm).
LACE FOR DRESS:
    Skirt: 2 pieces 5/8in (1.6cm) x 49in (124.4cm) each.
    Frill Caps: 5/8in (1.6cm) x 2yds.
    Sleeve ruffle: 1in (2.5cm) x 18in (45.7cm).

CUTTING INSTRUCTIONS

C1. LINING: Cut 1 bodice front, 2 bodice backs and 2 sleeve linings.
C2. DRESS BODICE: Cut 1 bodice front and 2 bodice backs, 1 facing (on fold if possible), 2 sleeves, 2 small frill caps and 2 large frill caps.
C3. DRESS SKIRT: Cut 1 rectangle measuring 10½in (26.7cm) x 40in (101.6cm). If skirt is to be tucked with 1/4in (0.65cm) tucks, cut a rectangle 11½in (29.2cm) x 40in (101.6cm).

Finished length of skirt, 8½in (21.6cm).
*Abbreviations: CB=center back and CF=center front.

ASSEMBLY INSTRUCTIONS
DRESS BODICE AND LINING

(1/4in [0.65cm] seam allowances unless otherwise noted.)

A1. Machine-stitch two rows of gathering stitches as shown on pattern of bodice front and bodice backs.
A2. Pleat as shown, the pleated areas at shoulders and necks on front bodice and back bodices. Tack in place. Place bodice dress front on bodice front lining, adjusting pleats slightly to fit lining if necessary; baste across neckline, shoulders and armseye. See *Illustration 1A*. Repeat for bodice backs.

FLUTING

A3. Using the technique described on page 83 of *Antique Children's Fashions*, for fluting, FLUTE the full section of the front and back bodice, gently pulling the fluting pleats toward center front or center back. This will set the fabric in a lovely rippled effect when it is gathered in at the waistline. See *Illustration 1A*.

A4. Match shoulder seams, center backs and center front; pin and stitch, leaving fullness at waistline loose. Matching center backs and center front, pull gathering stitches to fit lining, again holding gathered area at a slight angle toward center front or center backs. Baste in place. *See Illustration 1A.*

A5. Place dress bodice on doll OVER all UNDERWEAR and check fit. See page 68 of *Antique Children's Fashions,* paragraph two. Fold center back on fold lines or as fitting indicates, and tack to form closure (placket).

NECK FACING

A6. Lay facing around neckedge, right sides together. Machine-stitch all around. CLIP at corners; turn facing to inside; turn edges and tack in place.

SLEEVE Note: Sleeve lining is considerably smaller than the top sleeve. This will reduce bulk and make it easier to fit the sleeve into the armseye. This construction will provide beautiful blousing, and hems the sleeve at the same time.

A7. Machine-stitch gathering stitches on top and bottom of dress-top sleeve as shown on pattern.

A8. Place sleeve *bottom* edges together, *sleeve top RIGHT side* on sleeve lining WRONG side, matching seam ends. Pull gathering stitches of top sleeve to fit lining, distributing gathers evenly and machine-stitch.

A9. Place sleeve side seams together with sewn seam OUT; machine-stitch and press open. Flip dress top sleeve up and over seam forming a hidden hemline which puffs softly outward. Side seam is also hidden. *See Illustration 2.*

A10. Matching all notches on sleeve top and lining, pin in place; then pull gathering stitches to fit lining. Distribute gathers evenly and machine-stitch or hand-stitch in place. You now have a completed sleeve ready to set into armseye.

A11. Matching notches place sleeves in armseye, fitting carefully. See page 67, No. 2, and page 68, No. f, in *Antique Children's Fashions.* If necessary any slight additional fullness may be held in where gathering stitches are located (NOT in underarm area).
NOTE: A ruffle of lace may be added at the sleeve bottom seam. Lace about 1in (2.5cm) wide will make an attractive ruffle showing below the puff.

BACK CLOSURE

A12. Place dress top on doll; check again for correct overlap; sew hooks and threaded loops at neck edge and 1in (2.5cm) below first hook. Threaded loops should be sewn 1/4in (0.65cm) from folded edge. Do not add hook at the waistline until the skirt has been attached. See page 81, *Illustration 31* in *Antique Children's Fashions* for sewing loops.

SKIRT Note: If tucks and lace trim are desired, see Instruction No. A17 before starting gathers; check to see that the correct size rectangle for the skirt was cut.

A13. Machine-stitch two rows of gathering stitches on one long end of skirt, stopping gathering stitches about 1in (2.5cm) from center backs. Seam skirt center back edges from hemline to 3in (7.6cm) from waistline. Open seam and press; turn and hem by hand last 3in (7.6cm) to form a placket.

ATTACHING SKIRT TO BODICE

A14. With WRONG sides together, match center front of skirt to center front of LINING only; do not catch dress top in stitching, and match center backs. (Note that this will result in a seam toward the outside of the dress, but this will be covered by the bodice top. Machine-stitch skirt to dress lining and tack seam allowance in place upward.)

A15. Pull gathering stitches of bodice top to fit waistline; turn under the seam allowance, covering up all cut edges. Position bodice top carefully and hand-stitch in place. (This method should result in holding the "puff" out at the waistline.) Sew one hook and threaded loop at waistline.

HEM

A16. Place dress on doll over underwear and petticoat. See directions on page 67, No. 7 of *Antique Children's Fashions* for completing hem. After hemline has been determined (hem should be about 1½in (3.8cm), turn 1/4in (0.65cm) and hem BY HAND using a convenient hemming stitch. See above mentioned reference, page 80.

SKIRT TRIM

A17. LACE.

a. Mark a line along skirts 4in (10.2cm) from bottom. Using 5/8in (1.6cm) lace which is slightly gathered or slightly flared (see page 115 of *Antique Children's Fashions, Illustration 118* for shaping lace), place on marked line with scalloped edges down. Baste in place with small stitches.

b. TUCK. Make a fold 1/4in (0.65cm) above top of lace and press. Sew a 1/4in (0.65cm) tuck by machine, or hand-stitch along top edge of lace, just barely catching lace. Press tuck downward but do not flatten lace.

c. Repeat this process for a second row of lace and a second tuck, starting 1in (2.5cm) above the STITCHING of the first tuck.

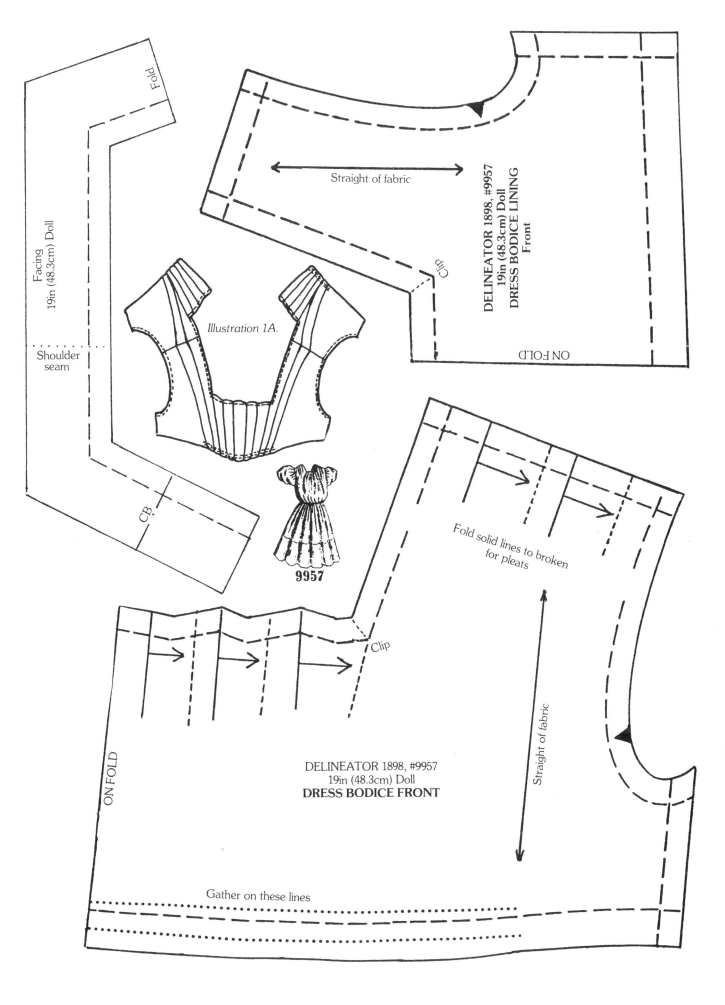

Fold

Facing
19in (48.3cm) Doll

Shoulder
seam

C.B.

Illustration 1A.

Straight of fabric

DELINEATOR 1898, #9957
19in (48.3cm) Doll
DRESS BODICE LINING
Front

Clip

ON FOLD

9957

Fold solid lines to broken
for pleats

Clip

Straight of fabric

ON FOLD

DELINEATOR 1898, #9957
19in (48.3cm) Doll
DRESS BODICE FRONT

Gather on these lines

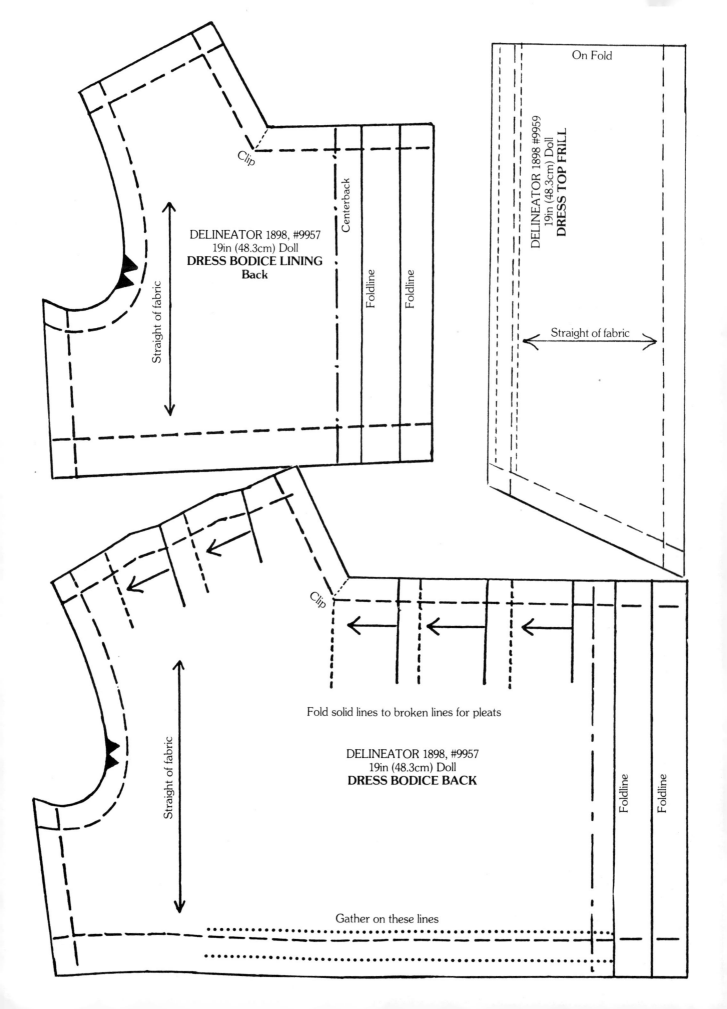

DELINEATOR 1898, #9957
19in (48.3cm) Doll
DRESS BODICE LINING
Back

Clip

Centerback

Foldline

Foldline

Straight of fabric

On Fold

DELINEATOR 1898 #9959
19in (48.3cm) Doll
DRESS TOP FRILL

Straight of fabric

Clip

Fold solid lines to broken lines for pleats

DELINEATOR 1898, #9957
19in (48.3cm) Doll
DRESS BODICE BACK

Straight of fabric

Foldline

Foldline

On Fold

Gather on these lines

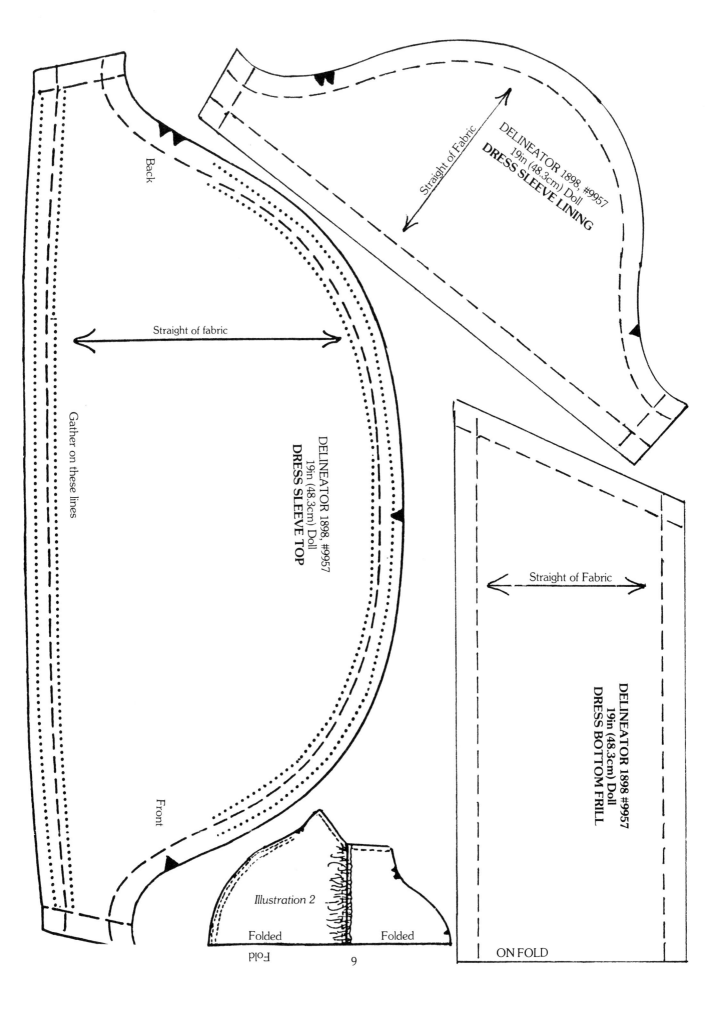

DELINEATOR 1898, #9957
19in (48.3cm) Doll
DRESS SLEEVE LINING

Straight of Fabric

Back

Straight of fabric

Gather on these lines

DELINEATOR 1898, #9957
19in (48.3cm) Doll
DRESS SLEEVE TOP

Front

Straight of Fabric

DELINEATOR 1898 #9957
19in (48.3cm) Doll
DRESS BOTTOM FRILL

Illustration 2

Folded   Folded

Fold

ON FOLD

9

FRILL CAPS

A18. HEM frills:

a. With a tiny hand stitch hem around three sides as shown on pattern. For help with tiny hems see page 115 of *Antique Children's Fashions*, first entry at top of page.

or

b. Line with sheer lining, stitching around three sides as shown, turning inside out and press.

A19. Add lace around three finished edges.

A20. Place one small frill over a large frill, matching raw edges and ends, and baste. Turn raw edges under 3/8in (0.9cm) and press or baste. Machine-stitch two rows of gathering stitches, one as close to the fold as possible, and one about 1/4in (0.65cm) from the folded edge. Matching one edge of frills to front neckline and one edge of frills to back neckline, pull gathering stitches to fit snugly over shoulder. Pin and then tack in place. Repeat for second frill.

SASH

A21. A sash of narrow ribbon may be added at the waistline if desired,

or

ROSETTES may be placed at corners of neckline and/or bows at waistline. See page 94 of *Antique Children's Fashions* for instructions for making rosettes. These may also be used as trim on bonnet.

VICTORIAN BONNET
1898

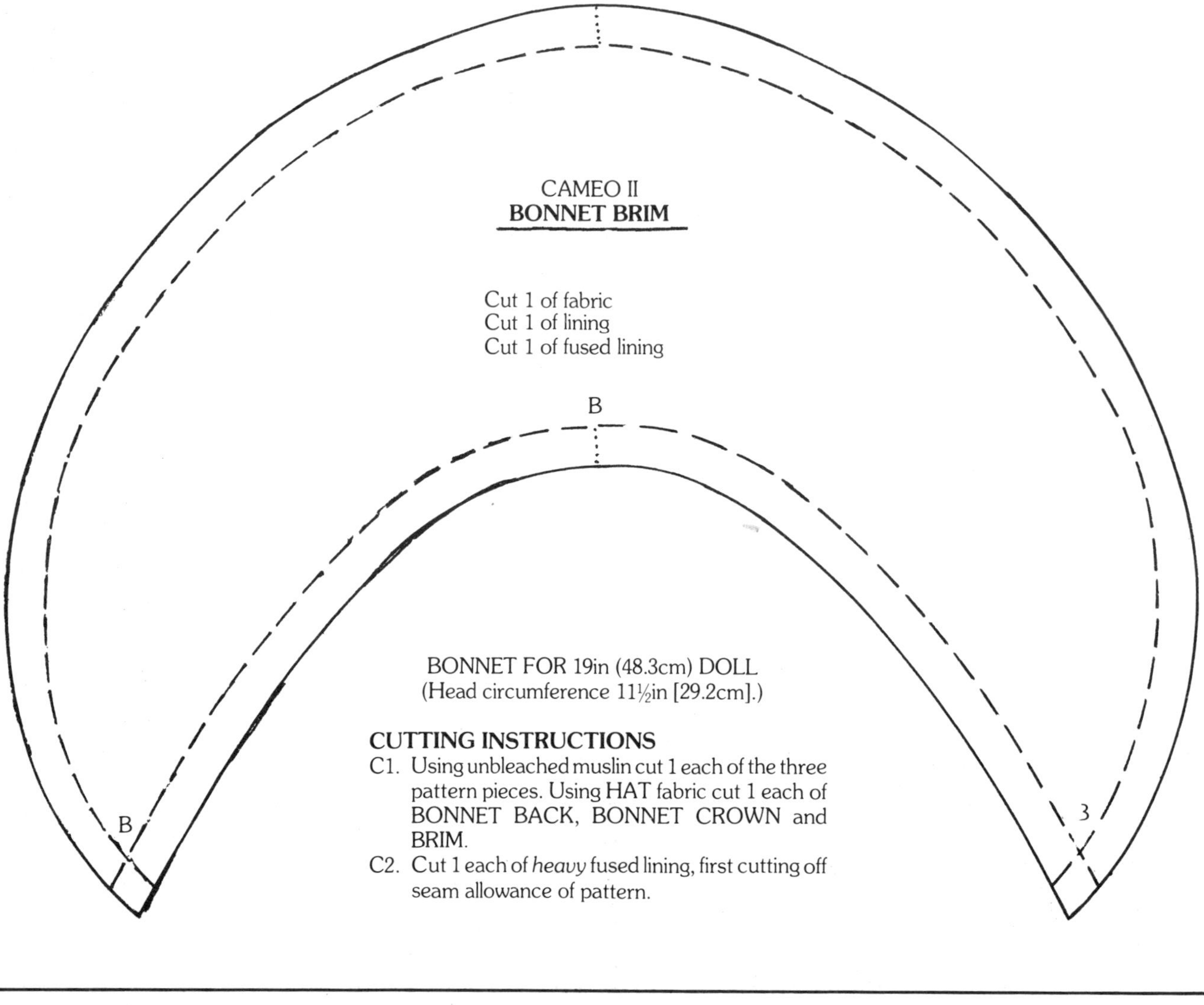

CAMEO II
BONNET BRIM

Cut 1 of fabric
Cut 1 of lining
Cut 1 of fused lining

B

B

3

BONNET FOR 19in (48.3cm) DOLL
(Head circumference 11½in [29.2cm].)

CUTTING INSTRUCTIONS

C1. Using unbleached muslin cut 1 each of the three pattern pieces. Using HAT fabric cut 1 each of BONNET BACK, BONNET CROWN and BRIM.

C2. Cut 1 each of *heavy* fused lining, first cutting off seam allowance of pattern.

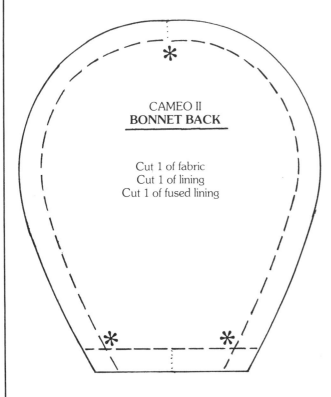

CAMEO II
BONNET BACK

Cut 1 of fabric
Cut 1 of lining
Cut 1 of fused lining

A3. CROWN: Place fused lining and fabric right sides together and sew 1/4in (0.65cm) from edge (next to fusing) along front edge. Turn right sides out and press. Sew ruching 1/4in (0.65cm) from finished edge. See page 92, *Illustration 61* in *Antique Children's Fashions* for information about ruching.

A4. BONNET BACK: Place bonnet back over lining and baste together.

A5. ASSEMBLE: Matching *s, sew bonnet back and crown together, pressing seam frontward with fingers. Bind neck edge with 1in (2.5cm) bias.

A6. Matching B's (marked on pattern), hand-stitch brim to crown. It is wise to start at center and sew to each side as brim tends to shift in the sewing process.

A7. Using 1in (2.5cm) ribbon, tack along brim to cover raw edge. Add ties and looped bows of ribbon at points R, and trim with small flowers or looped ribbon trim. Ties require 3/4yd (68.5cm) of ribbon. Check dress pattern A21 for information about rosettes, and *Cameo II,* page 14 for looped ribbon trim.

ASSEMBLY INSTRUCTIONS

A1. Fuse each lining piece to corresponding bonnet fabric piece. If desired, zigzag one or two strands of floral wire along bonnet BRIM edge of fused lining.

A2. BONNET BRIM:

a. Put corresponding fabric piece on fused piece of bonnet brim. Baste together. Using a bias of bonnet fabric, bind outer edge of brim.

b. SHIRRING FOR BRIM: Using English net or sheer silk, cut a rectangle 3½in (8.9cm) x 30in (76.2cm). Fold 1/2in (1.3cm) down on long edge and machine-stitch two rows of gathering stitches, one row 1/4in (0.65cm) from fold and one row 3/8in (0.9cm) from fold. Machine-stitch another row of gathering stitches 1¼in (3.2cm) from fold.

c. Matching centers, place shirring on front brim. Pull two rows of gathering stitches to fit brim and tack in place along brim. Pull third row of gathering stitches to fit brim. Set remaining fabric in tiny pleats along lower edge of brim, pulling gently so that shirring fits, surplus hanging free. Machine-stitch or hand-stitch in place and trim off surplus shirring.

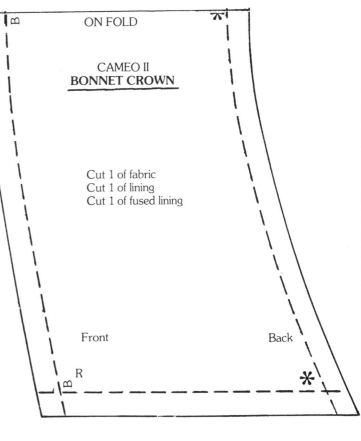

ON FOLD

CAMEO II
BONNET CROWN

Cut 1 of fabric
Cut 1 of lining
Cut 1 of fused lining

Front

Back

SITTING TEDDY BEARS

MATERIALS REQUIRED:

1. Small pieces of felt in brown or white.
2. Pipe cleaners.
3. Tiny black shiny eyes from a craft shop, about 1/8in (0.31cm) in diameter.

INSTRUCTIONS:

1. Cut 2 fronts and cut 1 back on a fold.
2. Machine or hand-stitch center front seam. Turn seam inward.
3. Place back and front *wrong* sides together. Hand sew with whipped stitches, very tiny, around head and arms.
4. Fold a pipe cleaner to fit tightly the outstretched arms and place into arms across body.
5. Stuff head and arms tightly with polyester filling.
6. Continue sewing body together leaving about 2in (5.1cm) open at bottom of body.
7. Repeat No. 5 for legs, making sure that pipe cleaner fits tightly.
8. Close bottom opening with hand-stitches.
9. Embroider snout with six-strand embroidery floss in approximately this pattern, altering to fit size of bear.
10. Glue on black eyes.
11. Bend arms and bend legs to desired position so that bear will sit.
12. Tie red ribbon around bear's neck.

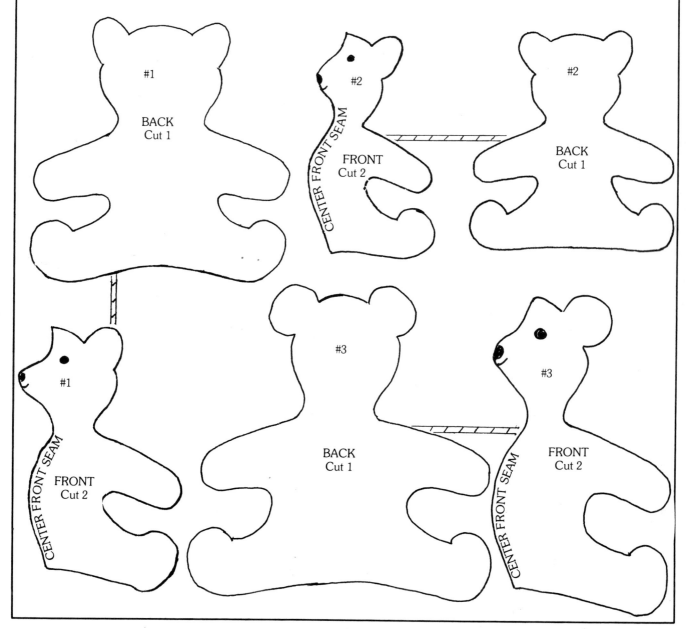

ANOTHER EASY BOW

ANOTHER PERFECTLY EASY TAILORED BOW

DRESS BOW for 23in (58.4cm) doll (slightly "drooped").

Ribbon required: 3/4yd (68.6cm) about 3in (7.6cm) or 3¼in (8.3cm) wide. From this
   length cut 18in (45.7cm) for a bow and two ties, 1-4in (2.5-10.2cm) long, and
   another 5in (12.7cm). Glue edges to prevent fraying, a process described in
   Antique Children's Fashions. See hints on page 116.

CONSTRUCTION:
1. Tie loose knot in exact center of the 18in (45.7cm) length of ribbon you have cut.
2. Run gathering stitch along one end of ribbon; turn toward back of knot and pull
   gathering stitches to fit knot. Slide gathered end under knot. Tack in place.
3. Turn remaining end back and slide under knot.
4. To get the VERY IMPORTANT "rounded or droopy" bow, pull loops down gently and
   tack at lower edge of knot.
5. Pleat end of ties to half the width and sew to back of bow as illustrated. Ends may be
   fringed or cut at an angle.

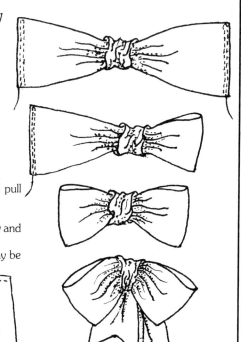

PAPER DOLLS

..I WANT TO BUY A PAPER DOLLY I CAN CALL MY OWN..

Did your grandmother or mother show you how they made paper dolls when they were little girls? No? Well, we will. Here goes...
   The old fashioned art of cutting paper dolls in strips can still provide hours of fun for little girls..and boys..and their elders can use extra skill in fashioning them for table settings around maypoles, for coloring or for other decorative purposes. Here we offer you a girl, a boy, a teddy bear and a bunny. From this point take off on your own. The sky is the limit.

1. Get a piece of construction paper 5in (12.7cm) x 16in (40.6cm). For BOY
   and GIRL rule the paper in 2in (5.1cm) strips, for *whole* doll. Fold on lines,
   alternating folds back and forth. See illustration. Trace pattern and cut,
   maintaining folds. Segments may be folded 1in (2.5cm) wide and one-half
   the pattern can be traced for cutting. For teddy bear use folded segments
   1½in (3.8cm) wide. For bunny use folded segments 1¼in (3.2cm) wide.

   Be sure to maintain folds and cut carefully. And voila! Paper dolls in a strip.
   Or paper teddy bears, or paper whatever.

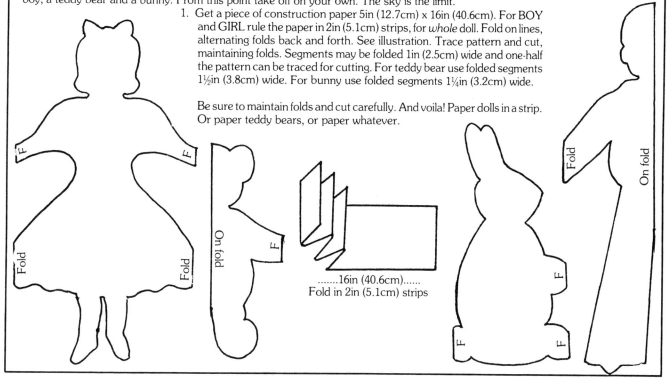

.......16in (40.6cm)......
Fold in 2in (5.1cm) strips

BONNET TRIMS

LOOPED RIBBON

1. Using 1in (2.5cm) ribbon, mark a length of ribbon into two 1/2in (1.3cm) segments and gather with thread at marks. Mark bonnet area to be trimmed at 1/4in (0.65cm) segments. (1¾yd [159.9cm].)

   Secure ribbon to bonnet. Tack 1/4in (0.65cm) segment permitting excess ribbon to stand up in a soft loop and continue in this manner across bonnet.

VARIATION: Instead of using two 1/2in (1.3cm) segments, as you become more expert, loops may be graduated on a bonnet for a 19in (48.3cm) doll so that the center loops gradually are made in segments up to 3½in (8.9cm) long, and then decreasing in size to the 1¾in (4.5cm) starting size.

   Ribbon width should be varied according to the size of the bonnet being trimmed.

For example:

1/2in (1.3cm) ribbon, 2in (5.1cm) loops, set at 1/4in (0.65cm) intervals.

1/4in (0.65cm) ribbon, 1½in (3.8cm) loops, at 1/8in (0.31cm) intervals.

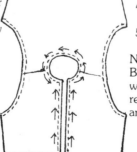

FLOWERS

a. Be sure flowers are in scale to size of bonnet; that is, 1/2in (1.3cm) flowers or smaller for dolls under 21in (53.3cm) in height, and not much larger for dolls over that size.

b. *Group* flowers, if there are not enough to cover a large area. DO NOT scatter a few flowers over a large area.

If you do not have enough flowers to cover a certain area, select a spot where good balance is achieved, and mass the flowers attractively in that area. Fill in on either side with ribbon...see looped ribbon, for example, or consider knotted ribbon.

KNOTTED RIBBON

Where ribbon is being placed on a curved line, as where brim meets crown, it will not lie flat. Solve this problem in an attractive way by knotting ribbon at intervals, depending on width of ribbon, the knots remaining loose, and tack in place.

SLIP TOP

INSTRUCTIONS FOR A LINED SLIP TOP

Particularly on tiny garments made of sheer cotton, we have found it difficult to finish edges securely. The following instructions may be used for any size, requiring only that 2 bodice fronts be cut, and 4 bodice backs.

1. Using 1 front section and 2 backs, sew shoulder seams. Press.
2. Using the second set of 1 front and 2 backs, sew shoulder seams. Press.
3. With right sides of the two assemblies together, match shoulder seams, side seams and center backs. Starting at waistline center back, sew up both center backs to neckline, and then sew around neckline. Clip to stitching around neckline; turn inside out, one top fitting into the other, thus showing a finished neckline and center back in one operation.
4. Sew sideseams. Place on doll to check neckline for snug fit, and for amount of overlap for plackets.
5. Trim around neckline with narrow lace if desired. Turn tiny hem around armseyes.

NOTE: Armseyes may be sewn in same operation. Before turning inside out, sew armseyes. Turn by working center back sections through front, which will result in completely finished edges for armseyes, neckline and center backs.

HINT FOR SEWING CROTCH SEAM OF DRAWERS

Before seaming at center back, turn center back edge twice 1/8in (0.31cm) and machine-stitch, forming a small hem. When center back seam is sewn, press open and hand-stitch from the machine-sewn seam to top to complete placket. This saves much frustration, particularly on small garments on which this bias cut edge is so likely to fray.

SHOES

LEATHER SLIPPERS FOR A 19" DOLL (copied from an old Jumeau shoe). Two sizes are shown, both for a 19" doll but slightly different in size.)

MATERIALS REQUIRED:
1. Small pieces of glove leather or heavy leather (one wrist-length glove makes one pair of shoes.)
2. Unbleached muslin.
3. Cardboard for inner sole, preferably of heavy cardboard from a pad of paper, and a dark manila folder for the outer sole, or very firm leather.
4. Glue, etc.

GENERAL INSTRUCTIONS:
Leather is an ideal medium for shoes as it is pliable, and elastic, and strong. Also we associate leather with good antique shoes.
A few hints are given for working with glove leather, a few for heavy leather.
1. Glove leather needs a lining, while heavy leather does not.
2. Patterns are given for both heavy leather and glove leather, since use of a lining requires a different-sized pattern.
3. When working with heavy leather, optional: machine-stitch around top of upper as close to edge as possible with matching thread, for a finished edge.

FITTING:
These patterns are both for 19in (48.cm) Jumeaus, but vary somewhat in size, so select the size nearest the size of your doll's feet. Shoes should be about 1/2in (1.3cm) longer than foot.
If you are willing to work a little harder for a good fit, try the sole pattern on the doll's foot and enlarge or reduce the pattern slightly to fit. Toes are slightly rounded. Doll shoes do not have a "left" and a "right" foot (in fact "human" shoes did not have left and rights until after mid-nineteenth century,) So be sure pattern is symmetrical.

CUTTING: (both kinds of leather)
SOLES:
1. Cut 4 soles the same size, 2 from light cardboard, 2 from thicker cardboard.

2. Cut 2 soles of unbleached muslin 1/4in (0.65cm) wider all around than sole pattern.
3. Spread glue evenly on two inner soles, place muslin over cardboard, smooth it out and glue muslin edges over soles.

UPPERS, GLOVE LEATHER
4. Cut 2 front uppers, and 4 back uppers, and corresponding linings of unbleached muslin. Spread a light layer of glue on lining and glue to wrong side of corresponding leather pieces.

UPPERS, HEAVY LEATHER. Broken line indicates lining.
5. Cut 2 front uppers and 4 back uppers. Machine-stitch around top of uppers.

ASSEMBLY:
1. With right sides together sew by hand with tiny overcast stitches front upper to back uppers, forming two side seams. Repeat for center back seams.
2. GLOVE LEATHER ONLY. Spread a light layer of glue on leather tops and around straps (NOT sole edge at this point) and roll leather over muslin holding in place with fingers until glue sets, thus forming a neatly finished edge.
   BOTH PATTERNS. Using doll's foot as a last, place inner sole on doll's foot with muslin side against the sole, holding in place with a rubber band. Put shoe upper on foot, securing straps. Fold upper over innersole, just enough to achieve good fit, and pin through leather to inner sole. Apply glue to inner sole to hold leather in place, press in place with fingers, smoothing out wrinkles. Allow to dry. Fill
3. in sole with leather scraps so it will be level.
4. Apply glue to outer sole, and press in place, holding till glue is set.

CLOSURE:
HEAVY LEATHER: Sew buttons at ends of straps, and secure with elastic loops.
GLOVE LEATHER: Pattern is designed so shoe can be buttoned near center of instep.

1886.
Styles for Little Folks.

Front View.

Front View.

CHILD'S DRESS.—Pattern No. **914**

914
Back View.

905
Back View.

CHILD'S COSTUME No. **905**

Front View.

Front View.

CHILD'S DRESS.—Pattern No. **913**

913
Back View.

920
Back View.

BOYS' COSTUME.—Pattern No. **920**.